How (not) to Save the World

THE TRUTH ABOUT REVEALING GOD'S LOVE TO THE PEOPLE RIGHT NEXT TO You

STUDY GUIDE ✚ FIVE SESSIONS

HOSANNA WONG

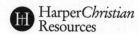 HarperChristian Resources

How (Not) to Save the World Study Guide

© 2022 by Hosanna Wong

Requests for information should be addressed to:

HarperChristian Resources, 3900 Sparks Dr. SE, Grand Rapids, Michigan 49546

ISBN 978-0-310-15122-7 (softcover)
ISBN 978-0-310-15123-4 (ebook)

HarperChristian Resources titles may be purchased in bulk for church, business, fundraising, or ministry use. For information, please e-mail ResourceSpecialist@ChurchSource.com.

Published in association with literary agent Jenni Burke of Illuminate Literary Agency, www.illluminateliterary.com.

First Printing June 2022 / Printed in the United States of America

Contents

Welcome to This Study!

When it comes to talking about Jesus and sharing the hope found in Him with our loved ones, our family members, friends, classmates, coworkers . . . many of us aren't sure we know how to do it. We don't want to come off as awkward, pushy, or straight-up weird. We wonder if we have the right words or if we'll say the wrong thing. So sometimes, we give up on sharing about Jesus altogether.

Yet, we live in a world that desperately needs hope—especially the hope found in Christ!

I've spent far too many years of my life believing lies about sharing my faith. I thought I had to do something impressive in order to do something impactful. I thought I had to have all the answers before I talked about God. I convinced myself that *other* people are called to share about Jesus—but I'm not smart enough, skilled enough, or spiritual enough to seal the deal. I thought my story was too different for people to relate to, or not different enough to actually make a difference. Rather than make a massive, muddy mess by talking about God, I thought it would be better if I just said nothing at all.

Maybe you've believed some of those lies, too. It turns out, believing all those lies? That's the perfect plan for how *not* to save the world. It's the surefire way to *not* show the hope of Jesus to a world that so desperately needs it. The truth is better.

What I've been discovering is the freedom and joy that comes with simply loving the people right in front of us. What the Bible actually says about sharing the love of God is far different than what I used to believe. It actually empowers us to become people who fight for others, who can naturally talk about Jesus through our real-life stories, and who can create meaningful relationships wherever we are.

In the upcoming sessions, we're going to crush the lies that have held us back from sharing the most important story in the world. We're going to dive deep into what God's Word actually says about revealing God's love in our day and age. And we're going to reignite our passion to reach those who don't know yet how much God loves them.

The truth? It is *more* than possible for you to naturally share God's love in your everyday life. There *is* a way for every person you know to realize how valuable he or she is to God. You've been created for it, equipped for it, and you're ready . . . let's go!

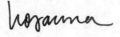

How To Use This *Guide*

Overview

How (Not) to Save the World Bible study curriculum is divided into five sessions. Every session includes Opening Discussion, Video Notes, Group Discussion Questions, Call to Action, Closing Prayer, and Between Sessions Personal Study. As a group, you should plan to discuss the opening questions, watch the video, and then use the video notes and questions to engage with the topic. You have complete freedom to decide how best to use these elements to meet the needs of your members. The goal is developing genuine relationships and becoming better equipped to share the good news of God's love with others—not just covering all the material.

Group Size

This five-session video Bible study is designed to be experienced in a group setting such as a Bible study, Sunday school class, retreat, or other small-group or online gatherings. If your gathering is large, you may want to consider splitting everyone into smaller groups of five to eight people. This will ensure that everyone has enough time to participate in discussions.

Materials Needed

Everyone in your group will need a copy of this study guide, which includes streaming video access located on the inside front cover. Videos are also available on DVD and by individual session download.

You will find opening questions to discuss, notes for the video teachings, directions for activities and discussion questions, and personal studies between sessions.

Facilitation

Your group will need to appoint a person to serve as a facilitator. This person will be responsible for starting the video and keeping track of time during discussions and activities. Facilitators may also read questions aloud and monitor discussions, prompting everyone in the group to respond and ensuring that everyone has an opportunity to participate.

Personal Studies

During the week, you can maximize the impact of this course with the personal studies provided. Treat each personal study like a devotional and use it in whatever way works best for your schedule. You could do a partial section each day or complete the personal study all in one sitting. These personal studies are not intended to be burdensome or time-consuming but to help you apply the lessons learned and discussed to your everyday, personal life for growth and connection.

Revealing God's Love through *Relationships*

The salvation of your family, your workplace, and your city is not all on you. Jesus is the One who saves lives, who heals marriages, who sets people free from addictions, and who makes the impossible possible . . . We are neither the climax of the story, nor the main point. Jesus is the subject, and we are the storytellers.

—Hosanna Wong
From Chapter 1 of *How (Not) to Save the World*

Opening Discussion

1. When you first encountered God, what circumstances and people were involved?

2. How would your life be different if no one had helped you encounter or grow in your relationship with God?

3. On a scale of one to ten, check the box that describes how easy it is for you to talk about God with others.

It's hard for me to talk about God with others.

It's easy for me to talk about God with others.

4. What are the biggest challenges or insecurities you face when sharing your faith?

Session 1 Video (18 minutes)

As you watch, take notes on anything that stands out to you.

NOTES:

▶ The first time you saw something broken that you wanted to fix

▶ We can talk about Jesus without fear of what the end results might be

▶ Lie: Only some people are called to share Jesus

▶ Jesus made friends first

▶ Our call is to be like Jesus, not to save, but to serve

▶ Mrs. Lee—make the invitation

> Hosanna opens with a powerful story of feeling powerless to help someone. She confesses, "At an early age, I believed the lie that as a Jesus follower, it was my duty to save everyone. But the truth is that it's not any of our jobs to save. We are not created to carry the weight of everyone's salvation on our shoulders. It's actually amazing news that Jesus is the savior and we're not."

1 **In which areas of your life do you struggle most with having a savior complex that reinforces the idea that everything relies on you? Check all that apply.**

____ Providing financial stability

____ Maintaining peace in relationships

____ Making everyone happy

____ Raising remarkable kids

____ Finding the right partner

____ Always volunteering when there's a need

____ Making your business thrive

____ Keeping the lawn or house perfect

____ Caring for an aging parent

____ Other: _____

2 Like Hosanna, can you identify a moment from your childhood that made you believe that everything depended on you? Share the circumstance or story with the group and discuss the effect it had on you.

3 All of us are susceptible to believing lies that hold us back from telling others about Jesus. Read through the list below and mark any of the following that have prevented you from sharing your faith.

- ◯ I need to be a perfect example of a Christian before I can share my faith.

- ◯ I need to have all the spiritual answers before I start the discussion.

- ◯ I'm afraid of being awkward, weird, or pushy.

- ◯ I've seen people share their faith using fear-based tactics and manipulation, and I don't want to be part of that.

- ◯ I don't have an impressive story of faith, so they won't listen to me.

- ◯ My story is too different, so they won't relate.

- ◯ My story is not different enough, so it won't make an impact.

- ◯ I've tried to share my faith in the past and it didn't work, so it won't work now.

- ◯ Other people are called to this, not me.

- ◯ Other people are gifted in this, not me.

- ◯ Other _____

4 Which of these holds you back most from sharing your faith? Why?

5 What do you need to do to overcome your hesitation?

6 What is at risk if you don't overcome some of the fears or whatever holds you back?

Bible Study Connection

Group leader, read the following comments to the group and then read the associated Bible passage aloud, followed by further discussion questions.

In believing these kinds of lies or holding on to bad experiences from the past, we can miss all God wants to do in and through us here and now.

In the Gospel of Matthew, Jesus reached out to a tax collector. These people were the social pariahs, the snakes and snitches of their time, who took more money than they should from patrons. Some even over-taxed their own family members and betrayed friends to expand their financial gain. Yet, as we'll discover, Jesus was constantly making friends with people . . . even *before* they changed their behaviors.

Before they chose Jesus, Jesus chose them.

1 **Read Matthew 9:9–13.**

How does Jesus invite and interact with Matthew and others like Him? (hint: v. 9–10)

What surprises you most about Jesus' generosity toward those who don't know Him?

How do the Pharisees respond to Jesus' generosity? (hint: v. 11)

What surprises you most about Jesus' response to the Pharisees? (hint: v. 12–13)

How would our lives look differently if we understood that the call that comes from Jesus is not a call to make people more religious, but a call to have more relationships?

Matthew wasn't the only social scoundrel Jesus invited into relationship.

2 **Read Luke 19:1–9.**

What were the parallels in the way Jesus approached Zacchaeus and Matthew? (9:9–13)

What challenges you most about how Jesus reached out to others? What comes most naturally to you? What's the most difficult to embrace from this passage?

What practical tips can you take from these passages to help you share your faith with others?

3 **Hosanna tells the story of Mrs. Lee's interaction with a vacuum salesman. Despite the rough and tumble background of the man, Mrs. Lee responded without shock or shame. Instead of highlighting the ways their lives differed, she focused on what they had in common. Then she shared what Jesus had done for her. That man came to know Jesus. Years later, the former vacuum salesman introduced Hosanna, his daughter, to Jesus.**

In a nutshell, what has Jesus done in your life? If you were to paint the picture of your life before knowing Jesus and after knowing Jesus, how would you describe it?

4 **Who are three people who are right in front of you—on your street, in your apartment building, at school pick up, in a nearby cubicle, in your family, on a walking path—whom you've overlooked and can begin building relationships with? Name them here. No need to share names with the group.**

- _____
- _____
- _____

Discuss practical ways that you can make invitations, have conversations, and share your stories without fear of the result.

Call to Action

Team up with someone in your group (or online if you are doing this study virtually) and reveal the three names that you wrote in question 4. Share a little about each person with your partner, and take a moment to pray for opportunities to deepen the connection and talk naturally about Jesus when the time comes.

Conclusion

Group leader, read aloud to the group to close your time together this week.

The people in our lives whom we encounter, know, and love, are looking for hope and peace, and they need to know where it can be found. Every day we can help others discover how deeply loved they are. And it all begins with an authentic relationship.

Jesus never called us to save the world. He's already got that. Jesus calls us to serve the world. We can faithfully show up for people, develop real relationships, and naturally talk about our faith.

Closing Prayer

Select a volunteer to read the closing prayer over the group.

Free us from the lie that only some people are called to share the good news of Jesus. Help us see ourselves as your chosen vessels for the gospel to be heard by every person, everywhere. Give us opportunities to engage spiritually with people we meet and those already in our lives. May Your Spirit spark conversations. Give us the grace to focus more on what we have in common than any differences. Stir our hearts with Your deep affection and holy expectation. Amen.

Between Sessions

Personal Study

Check in with your group members during the upcoming week and continue the discussion you had with them at your last gathering. Grab coffee, dinner, or reach out by text and share what's going on in your life and heart. Use the following questions to help guide your conversation.

Sometimes to move forward, we need to identify what lies might be holding us back. Perhaps you've tried to talk about Jesus with a friend or family member and it didn't go well. Place a check mark by any of the following that you've experienced.

_____ I've tried to talk to others about Jesus, but I couldn't find the right words.

_____ I've tried to invite a friend to church or a small group, and they just won't come.

_____ I've tried to share about my faith, but it feels like their eyes just glaze over.

This week's group discussion is just the start, and the goal is to keep digging into how you can share God's love with the people right next to you. This section is created as a guide for your personal study time to further explore the topics you discussed with your group. If you're following along with the book for the fullest experience of this message, read or review chapters 1–3 in *How (Not) to Save the World*.

___ I've prayed for my child who is so far from God, and nothing has changed.

___ Other disappointment

_____

_____

_____

1 **In the space below, write a prayer asking God to heal your disappointments and to reignite your passion for prayer and sharing His love.**

_____

_____

_____

_____

_____

_____

_____

_____

_____

_____

Though we may want and ache for the very best for others, sometimes we feel the pressure of getting the results we desire on our timetable. We push faster and harder and find ourselves on a treadmill of trying to save, which often leaves us exhausted, frustrated, discouraged, and depleted.

We are not the first people who have noticed this world needs saving. The religious people of Jesus' day were also looking for a hero. They believed a king, a warrior, was coming to defeat the evil empires, fight off the tyrannical leaders, and forcefully turn over the corrupted governments of the day.

And Someone did come.

He had more power than they could ever comprehend, and yet He didn't come to take over with forceful power at all.

Instead, they were introduced to a Savior not participating in remarkable battles or lobbying for impressive titles to declare His status; no, He gave up His status. In a world where we naturally seek our own glory and applaud those whom we find glorious, we surprisingly find that the One who already had all the glory did not aim to be above us but came to be *with* us.

❷ Read Philippians 2:5–8. Describe how Jesus showed His love according to this passage.

What does it look like for you to live out Philippians 2:5–8 in a practical way?

What situations tempt you to believe the lie that you must be the savior?

3 Think through the difference between these two circumstances: *having to be a savior* or *looking for opportunities to be a servant.* Which gives you more freedom? What do you get out of each experience? Which circumstance do you find yourself experiencing most frequently? Explain.

How would your life be different if you stopped seeing the call to share Jesus as a rigid mandate to convert and instead saw it as the freedom to continuously have real relationships with those right next to you?

4 Read Luke 7:36–39. How does the woman who lived a sinful life show her affection for Jesus? What does this say about the woman?

5 Read Luke 7:40–43. What does Jesus reveal about the source of the woman's affection? What does Jesus' response to her reveal about what He considers most important?

6 Read Luke 7:44–50. How do the actions of the woman and the Pharisee compare?

WOMAN'S RESPONSE TO JESUS	PHARISEE'S RESPONSE TO JESUS

Based on this story, how do you think Jesus felt about being known as a friend of sinners? (Matthew 9:11)

What if the call that comes from Jesus is not a call to make people more religious, but a call to have more relationships? How would we live our lives differently?

When you choose to serve the world, instead of trying to save it, that means you can throw a dinner party and invite anyone. That means you can host a Bible study and not worry about how many people show up. That means you can reach out to coworkers to go to lunch and if they pass, it doesn't spiral you into thoughts of defeat. You're free to risk. You're free to reach out. You're free to have fun in your friendships.

You're free to embrace those on the margins. You're free to discover and seek out whom God just might bring into your life.

How can we *reveal* God's love in our everyday lives?

▶ **Make invitations.**
▶ **Have conversations.**
▶ **Share our stories.**

In chapter 2 of *How (Not) to Save the World*, "Go Big or Get Out," Hosanna writes the following reminder:

> *There is no training course we must graduate from in order to have lively relationships with those around us. There is no certificate we must have on our wall before we can serve those in need in our workplaces. We do not need to be biblical scholars in order to do real life with real people, ask honest questions, and give honest answers. As we give invitations and have conversations, cultivating commonality with those around us, we begin to know people—people God really loves. And people begin to know us. Like any ongoing friendship, as you are continuously honest and open, over time the most important things in your life naturally seep out in your conversations and through your actions. They will naturally discover who Jesus is to you, learning that He is a big deal in their friend's life, the reason their friend is joyful,*

kind, purpose-filled, and resilient. When you don't know where to start, remember: Everybody loves good food. And everybody loves good friends.

7 **How do Hosanna's assurances help you catch a fresh vision for how God might use you to spread His love and hope and provision to hurting people in a broken world?**

8 **What are a few ways you might be a "good friend" this week? Feel free to incorporate the "good food" part of the equation in your list too, you know, just to share.**

1.

2.

3.

4.

5.

9 **Before your next group meeting, read chapters 4—6 if you are reading along with the book.**

God's *Power,* Not Ours

The wonderful, freeing truth is that when I feel (God) directing, I don't have to wait for perfect, but I can go where I think He's leading and obey what I think He is saying. Sometimes I'll even get it right. But every time I step out in faith to obey, trust, and rely on Him, He loves that... And ultimately, either way, we get to spend that time together.

—Hosanna Wong
From Chapter 4 of *How (Not) to Save the World*

Opening Discussion

1 Describe a time when you felt a tug on your heart to share your faith. How did it go?

2 On a scale of one to ten, check the box that describes how much you feel like you're on your own and it's all up to you when you talk about God with others.

It feels like I'm	It feels like I'm
on my own	not alone when
when I talk about	I talk about God
God with others.	with others.

3 What role could prayer and dependence on the Holy Spirit play in changing your perspective?

Session 2 Video (21 minutes)

As you watch, take notes on anything that stands out to you.

NOTES:

▶ You work hard for God, but don't enjoy Him

▶ Lie: Rely on your own power

▶ Be filled with the Holy Spirit

▶ Rhythm of resting and retreat

▶ Story of campfire and sweet aroma

▶ Speak, Lord, I am listening

Group Discussion Questions

Hosanna opens with a story of her husband, Guy, helping her realize that while she was good at working hard for God, she didn't seem to enjoy God.

1 **On the continuum below, mark how much you struggle with being a productivity-focused or work-a-holic person.**

I don't struggle
at all.

It's an everyday
battle.

2 **With full disclosure and humility, share the ways in which you put effort into working for God. Where are you motivated by doing for the sake of doing rather than motivated by God's love for you to share with others? We cannot change until we are clear about from where we are beginning.**

3 **Place a check by any of the following ways you enjoy and rest in God.**

_____ Talk about God with others.

_____ Talk to God through prayer.

_____ Take a half-day or day of rest.

_____ Sing songs, dance, or create.

___ Meditate on a Scripture for its richness.

___ Simply be with God.

___ Hand over your concerns and worries.

___ Do a daily activity with God.

___ Invite the Holy Spirit's presence.

___ Enjoy God's creation.

___ Look for God's presence in surprising and delightful ways.

___ Other: _____

4 **Where are you most tempted to work for God rather than enjoy God?**

5 **What steps could you take this week to enjoy God more?**

6 **Which are you more drawn to: people who work hard for God or those who deeply know and enjoy God? Explain.**

Bible Study Connection

Group leader, read the following comments to the group and then read the associated Bible passage aloud, followed by further discussion questions.

In our homes, in our neighborhoods, in our cities, in our world, there are people from every nation who need to know the One who saves.

1 **Read Romans 10:9–15.**

How does someone experience salvation according to this passage? (hint: v. 9–13)

What role do you play in bringing the news of salvation? (hint: v. 14–15)

Jesus came to this world serving others. He lived in this world demonstrating how to serve others. After He died and rose again, He appeared multiple times and gave specific instructions to His followers.

2 **Read Matthew 28:18–20 and Acts 1:1–8.**

What instructions does Jesus give His followers? How do these instructions complement each other?

What's the role of the Holy Spirit in helping share the good news with others? (hint: Acts 1:8)

How do you personally sense the power of the Spirit in your life?

When do you tend to be most and least attentive to the Spirit's presence and power?

Hosanna teaches that Christ-following, Holy Spirit–filled people can draw people to Jesus. They bring the fragrance of God and His peace, love, and joy with them.

3 Read 2 Corinthians 2:14–15.

What is one of your favorite fragrances? (hint: freshly baked bread, a scented candle, freshly cut grass, etc.)

How do you bring the fragrance of Christ when you're walking in the power and presence of the Holy Spirit?

Being the aroma of Christ is tied to how we treat and how we respond to others. How can you be the aroma of Christ, creating an environment of encouragement, forgiveness, and reconciliation in each of the following situations?

- A family member disagreeing with you:

- An impatient driver who is riding your bumper:

- A person who rolls their eyes at the very mention of God:

- A church member who avoids you and refuses to make eye contact:

- A stranger who looks discouraged and beaten down:

4 **At the end of the group discussion for session 1, you were asked to list three people whom God has placed right in front of you for a possible new connection. Whom do you sense the Holy Spirit is prompting you to reach out to this week?**

Name them here. No need to share names with the group.

- _____

- _____

- _____

Discuss practical ways that you can ask and rely on the power of the Holy Spirit to make invitations, have conversations, and share your stories.

Call to Action

Team up with someone in your group (or online if you are doing this study virtually) and share the three names that you wrote in question 4. Tell a little about that person with your partner and take a moment to pray for the presence and the power of the Holy Spirit to create opportunities to connect and talk about Jesus.

Conclusion

Group leader, read aloud to the group to close your time together this week.

Our calling is not to spend more time working or producing for God, but to spend more time knowing and enjoying Him. We need to rest and be renewed in His presence and receive the power that comes through the Holy Spirit.

When we lean into the work of the Spirit, we no longer rely on our efforts, but come alongside what the Spirit is already doing. As our lives overflow with the fragrance of God, we naturally make people feel like they belong, they are loved, and there's something different about God and His people.

Closing Prayer

Select a volunteer to read the closing prayer over the group.

Free us from the lie that everything relies on us. Help us to grow in our enjoyment of you. Fill us with the presence and power of the Holy Spirit. Let us carry your fragrance to a lost and hopeless world. May we be people who are known by the fruit of the Spirit, demonstrate the love of Jesus, and lead others to Christ. Amen.

Between Sessions

Personal Study

Check in with your group members during the upcoming week and continue the discussion you had with them at your last gathering. Grab coffee, dinner, or reach out by text and share what's going on in your life and heart. Use the following questions to help guide your conversation.

When we surrender our lives to Jesus, we then belong to Him, and we are identified with Him. We discover more of whom we are when we sit in His presence, His Word, know Him, and talk to Him every day. We soon discover that the call that comes from Jesus isn't just a task to be accomplished, rather it's an invitation to know and to belong—and it begins with us knowing and belonging to God and being filled with the Holy Spirit.

This week's group discussion is just the start, and the goal is to keep digging into how you can share God's love with the people right next to you. This section is created as a guide for your personal study time to further explore the topics you discussed with your group. If you're following along with the book, read or review chapters 4-5 in *How (Not) to Save the World.*

1 **Read Ephesians 1:3-4. What spiritual blessings have been bestowed on you?**

What more do you need from God to share Jesus with others?

The power of the Holy Spirit produces a different kind of fruit in us than anything the world offers. People are naturally drawn to this fruit. No one ever hates being loved or having someone treat them kindly. No one ever shouts, "Stop being so patient with me!"

2 **Read Galatians 5:22–23. What are the facets of the fruit of the Spirit?**

Which of these comes most naturally to you? Which of these do you struggle with the most?

In the space below, write a prayer asking the Holy Spirit to grow the fruit you need most now.

_____

_____

_____

_____

_____

_____

_____

_____

_____

3 **Read Proverbs 6:16–19 (see callout). Circle or underline the things that the writer Solomon says God hates.**

> "There are six things the LORD hates, seven that are detestable to him: haughty eyes, a lying tongue, hands that shed innocent blood, a heart that devises wicked schemes, feet that are quick to rush to evil, a false witness who pours out lies and a person who stirs up conflict in the community."
> —Proverbs 6:16-19

On the grid below, list the things that God hates in the left-hand column. In the center column, list the opposite of the thing God hates—in other words, what He must *love*, based on what He hates. In the right-hand column, think of a simple, straightforward, totally-doable example of how a person could demonstrate the thing that God loves in everyday life.

	WHAT GOD HATES	WHAT GOD MUST LOVE	EVERYDAY EXAMPLE OF THE BEHAVIOR GOD LOVES
1			
2			
3			
4			
5			
6			
7			

If we're walking in the power and presence of the Spirit and carrying the fragrance of God with us, that means we can do it in person, as well as when we're emailing or texting, and when we're online.

When it comes to social media, we need to be intentional to *engage*. It's easy to scroll on our social media platforms and see people's life updates, baby photos, family losses, and big career moves, and fall into the comparison trap. Instead, we can take time to engage and see every person as someone we can cheer on, make feel seen, or speak life over.

We can also use social media to *encourage*. We can remind people of whom they are in Christ and shout out the moments we see them reflecting Jesus.

A lesser-known way to use social media is as an opportunity to *encounter God*. We can intentionally turn our feeds into prayer lists and use them to intercede for others.

4 **Rank the following 1–5, by how much you enjoy engaging with people through the following means.**

_____ In person _____

_____ Email _____

_____ Text _____

_____ Social Media or Online _____

_____ Phone call _____

Next to each method of engaging others, take a moment to pray and ask the Holy Spirit to bring someone to mind. Write (at least) one person's name next to each method of communication.

Now, considering how you can best engage with that person, pray for that person, and use whichever means to offer a word of encouragement or share your prayer for them.

⑤ Take 5–15 minutes and reach out to *each person.* Try to avoid getting distracted and stay focused on serving those on the list as you do this. That means you will have one meet up, one email, one text, one social shout out, and one phone call to make. This is not hard. This is good.

Jesus' mission for the saving of souls will absolutely require our *participation*—to *tell* the people in our lives what we love about Him—to *show* His kindness and compassion to them, so they know what He's like.

In chapter 4 of *How (Not) to Save the World,* "Wait for Perfect," Hosanna writes the following reminder:

> *I am encouraged by the apostle Paul, who told the church in Rome that "God is able to orchestrate everything to work toward something good and beautiful when we love Him and accept His invitation to live according to His plan" (Romans 8:28 VOICE). As I truly love God and actively live according to His ways, He is able to use every step I take and choice I make and put it toward something good and beautiful.*

On the continuum below, mark how easy or hard it is for you to trust that God can create something good and beautiful out of sharing your faith with others.

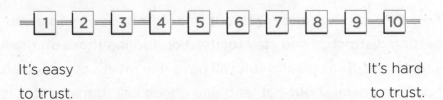

It's easy
to trust.

It's hard
to trust.

6 **In the space below, write a prayer asking God to do good and beautiful things as you deepen your relationships and share your faith.**

_____

_____

_____

_____

_____

_____

_____

_____

_____

7 **Before your next group meeting, read chapters 6–9 if you are reading along with the book.**

The *Power* of Your Story

I spent so much of my life trying to figure out whom I was supposed to be like that I didn't realize I was supposed to be more of whom I already was. I thought the details of my life were walls, but they were doors. These doors were helping me invite more people into the story of a redeeming Savior . . . God wanted to use my real story to reveal His real power. And He wants to use yours.

—Hosanna Wong
From Chapter 6 of *How (Not) to Save the World*

Opening Discussion

1 What are two details about your life that might surprise others (especially in the group) about you? Share the responses.

- _____

- _____

2 How did sharing these details help stir curiosity, connection, and conversation?

3 On a scale of one to ten, check the box that describes how easy it is for you to uncover details of other people's lives.

| 1 | 2 | 3 | 4 | 5 | 6 | 7 | 8 | 9 | 10 |

It's hard for me
to uncover details
about others.

It's easy for me
to uncover details
about others.

4 On a scale of one to ten, check the box that describes how easy i is for you to list and share the interesting details of your life.

| 1 | 2 | 3 | 4 | 5 | 6 | 7 | 8 | 9 | 10 |

It's hard for me
to share details
about my life.

It's easy for me
to share details
about my life.

5 Discuss which comes easier for you—finding the details of others' lives or sharing details from your own.

Session 3 Video (19 minutes)

As you watch, take notes on anything that stands out to you.

NOTES:

▶ I hated that I didn't fit in

▶ Lie: Silence your story

▶ God made you good

▶ You were made for good things

▶ You were made for the good of others

▶ God gives us the authority to make Him known

Group Discussion Questions

Hosanna opens by sharing with vulnerability how she tried to hide her features, her background, even her last name, from others.

1 **What is something in your background you try to hide or not share with others for fear of judgment or rejection?**

2 **How does this sharing this detail with the right people create connection, compassion, and authenticity?**

3 **When it comes to sharing your story of faith, circle the lies that are most tempting for you to believe.**

My story is not the right story.

My story isn't big enough.

My story doesn't have power.

My story is uninteresting.

No one cares to hear my story.

My story can't make much of an impact.

My story carries too much shame.

4 **How have you been tempted to stop or silence your story because of these lies?**

5 How have you been tempted to curate a false presentation of your story or pretend things are different than they truly are?

> Hosanna teaches, "God created you, your quirks, your story, your scars, your joys, your hobbies, your abilities, your limitations, your relationships, your background, where you're from, what you've overcome, what you've dreamed of, what you're passionate about, and what you despise. Every detail that makes you, you, God wants to use it. Anything you give Him, He will use. He's very eco-friendly like that. He doesn't waste one thing. Your details are your superpower!"

6 How have you seen this to be true in other people's stories?

7 What stops you from seeing this truth in your story?

Bible Study Connection

Group leader, read the following comments to the group and then read the associated Bible passage aloud followed by further discussion questions.

The truth is that you were made in God's image. You reflect Him. You have His image stamped on you. Unlike the other days of creation, God calls His creation on the sixth day *very* good.

1 **Read Genesis 1:26–31.**

Discuss anything that prevents you from believing you're the very good creation of God.

Not only are you made good, but you are also made for good things.

2 **Read Ephesians 2:10.**

What were you created to do?

In what ways is this easy for you to believe?

In what ways is this challenging to you now?

Not only are you made good, for good things, but you're also made for the good of others. It may be your availability on weeknights or your weird sense of humor that make your kids and their friends want to come over and hang out at your house after school. Those details about you are a good thing and they're opening a door. It may be your long log of handwritten recipes that allows you to start a baking and Bible study group, or your love of cars that helps you start an auto group where you share in this common interest and learn and study God's word together.

1 **Read 1 Peter 4:10–11.**

What's one gift you're confident God has given you to usher goodness into this world?

What holds you back from using that gift more often?

People need to hear about how God interacts in people's real lives so that they can know how God can interact in their real lives, too.

God often uses the hard things in our lives to help bring healing in other people's lives. The Apostle Paul uses the image of clay jars to remind us that we have this great hope, this great light inside of us. And it's through the cracks of our lives, those broken places, that God's mighty power is revealed.

2 **Read 1 Corinthians 4:7–10.**

Discuss one struggle or place of pain where you've encountered God's power, presence, or grace.

3 **How does sharing your story and hearing others' stories reveal Jesus' power and presence?**

4 **Why is it so important to keep sharing these real stories?**

Call to Action

Team up with someone in your group (or online if you are doing this study virtually) and share one brief story of God's goodness and faithfulness in your life. Take a moment to pray for opportunities to connect and share this story with others this week.

Conclusion

Group leader, read aloud to the group to close your time together this week.

Sometimes we're tempted to hide details about ourselves—our backgrounds and upbringings—to make our stories sound better. We can believe the lie that our story is not the right story. Yet, the truth is, you were made good, you were made for good things, and you were made for the good of others. The details of your story are your superpower.

The enemy wants to silence and stop you from telling your story and the ways God has revealed His love in and through you. You not only have permission, but the responsibility to use all that you are to share God's love and make His restoring power known. Jesus is the one who saves, and our stories are the proof.

Closing Prayer

Select a volunteer to read the closing prayer over the group.

God, we don't want to silence our stories or hide the details of our lives from others when they proclaim the proof of your power. Help us discover the details of others' stories and share our own, so we can communicate the depths of your love. Let us be the living proof of your goodness and grace. Give us new open doors to share our stories and yours. And give us the courage to walk through those doors when they open. Amen.

Between Sessions

Personal Study

Check in with your group members during the upcoming week and continue the discussion you had with them at your last gathering. Grab coffee, dinner, or reach out by text and share what's going on in your life and heart. Use the following questions to help guide your conversation.

Previous sessions explored the impact of making invitations and starting conversations. The challenge of sharing personal stories is where it can get complicated. Invitations and conversations can come naturally but talking about the past or confessing current struggles can be more challenging. Yet, it's often in talking about hard things that we bring healing and hope to others. This is evident in the story of Jesus and Lazarus.

1 **Read John 11:1–16. How does Jesus respond to the news of Lazarus' sickness?**

This week's group discussion is just the start, and the goal is to keep digging into how you can share God's love with the people right next to you. This section is created as a guide for your personal study time to further explore the topics you discussed with your group. If you're following along with the book for the fullest experience of this message, read or review chapters 6-9 in *How (Not) to Save the World.*

What surprises you most about Jesus' response?

What hope does Jesus have regarding Lazarus' death?
(hint: v. 4, 11, 15)

2 **Read John 11:17–25. How does Jesus use the pain of this incredible loss to reveal God's love and resurrection power?**

When have you experienced God's love and power amid pain or suffering?

③ Read John 11:26-37. How does Jesus express His compassion and love in this passage?

How does this reflect God's heart for you and all of humanity?

Some people don't understand what Jesus is about to do (v. 37). There will always be people who don't understand our stories or what we're going through. Yet, Jesus shows that these people should never hold us back.

4 **Read John 11:38-44. What compels Jesus in this passage? (hint: v. 38)**

What role does compassion play in listening to other people's stories and sharing your own?

Why does Jesus pray and perform this miracle? (hint: v. 41–42)

⑤ Read John 11:45–48. What did the religious leaders fear most from this powerful story?

These leaders were so afraid of this powerful story that they doubled-down on their resolve soon after.

6 Read John 12:9-11. What do the responses of the religious leaders reveal about the power of story and the resurrection power of Christ?

The circulating story of Lazarus was a direct threat to everything the enemy wanted to accomplish, which was to keep as many people as possible from discovering the truth about Jesus.

The enemy couldn't keep Jesus in the grave. So, the enemy's next best plan is to try to keep the proof of His power hidden. The enemy wants you to keep the victory that's found in Jesus buried. Yet, every time you tell stories of how God has changed, healed, renewed, and restored: you demonstrate the proof of God's power. You are the living proof that Jesus is alive!

How does your story confirm the life of Jesus?

How does silencing your story prevent others from hearing about Jesus?

7 **Read 1 Corinthians 1:4–6. How is God writing His story in you according to this passage?**

What hope does that give you in sharing your life story with others?

Keep the *evidence* of Christ's resurrection circulating, let your story be *heard*, and keep the proof of Jesus' power *alive*.

In chapter 6 of *How (Not) to Save the World*, "Silence Your Story," Hosanna writes the following reminder:

> *I'm not saying that showing the world Jesus will be easy. Not at all. I'm saying it will absolutely take your participation. It will likely take these three things: making invitations, having conversations, and sharing your story. It will take your real life being revealed, your actual details being shown, and your true story being told. Too much is at risk for us to hoard this message. For as long as we live, may the proof of Jesus Christ be seen, heard, and kept alive.*

8 **What's a fun activity that taps into your gifts and joys that you can invite someone to join you in this week?**

Go ahead, invite one person or several to join you!

9 **Before your next group meeting, read chapters 10–12 if you are reading along with the book.**

The Truth About *Community*

When the Creator of the universe first thought of us and hand-made us, He designed us to be in community—*with* God and *with* each other. Community is not an optional add-on in our Amazon cart that we can choose before we check out the main items. It's essential for our lives to reach their full potential. Community empowers us not only to complete the tasks God has called us to but to become the people He has made us to be.

—Hosanna Wong
From Chapter 10 of *How (Not) to Save the World*

Opening Discussion

1 When you think of being part of a community, which of the following words describe your experience?

___ Grace

___ Love

___ Hurt

___ Fun

___ Comfort

___ Betrayal

✓ Unity

___ Hope

___ Disappointment

___ Companionship

✓ Togetherness

___ Back-stabbing

___ Faith-building

___ Hardship

___ Loneliness

___ Other _____

2 On a scale of one to ten, check the box that describes how easy it is for you to be part of a community.

It's hard for me
to be part of
a community.

It's easy for me
to be part of
a community.

3 What are the biggest hurdles you face when it comes to being part of a community of believers?

4 How have your past experiences helped or hindered you from being part of a faith community now?

Session 4 Video (22 minutes)

As you watch, take notes on anything that stands out to you.

NOTES:

▶ God designed us to be in community

▶ Lie: You're better off doing life alone

▶ Say yes to invitations and make invitations

▶ Don't tear down the very community you're called to grow

▶ Redwoods

▶ God says we are better together

Group Discussion Questions

1 What are some of the greatest rewards and joys of being part of a community?

2 Describe a time when you experienced a community or group of people rallying around you in a time of need. What was most meaningful about this?

3 Describe a time when you were part of a community or group of people rallying around someone else in a time of need. What was most meaningful about this?

Hosanna teaches that two of the best ways to build relationships and become part of a community are to say *yes* to the invitations you're given and make invitations to others. (Remember, to keep it healthy, don't put pressure on every lunch date to be your lifelong confidant, your forever-ride-or-die friendship.)

4 What's an invitation from a group or person you could agree to try? (hint: check the activities at your church)

5 What's an invitation you could make to someone this week? (hint: look for people new to town or someone who has also mentioned it's hard to find connection)

6 What are best practices for growing friendships and becoming part of a community?

Bible Study Connection

Group leader, read the following comments to the group and then read the associated Bible passage aloud followed by further discussion questions.

On the night of His arrest, Jesus gathers His disciples in one place to be together and share a meal. Toward the end of the evening, He prays for His closest followers.

1 **Read John 17:20-23.**

What is Jesus' desire for His followers then and today?

Why do you think Jesus doesn't want us to go it alone?

What happens when you try to do life and faith all by yourself?

What message does it send to the world when believers live in love and unity? (hint: v. 23)

2 On the continuum below, mark how much the world needs to see believers fulfilling Jesus' prayer today.

They don't
need to see
love or unity.

They desperately
need to see
love or unity.

What changes in your attitudes, actions, or responses do you need to make to bring greater love and unity to your community of believers?

Living in love and unity is a bold witness to the world. Jesus was passionate about people and community and believed the church was the hope of the world. He called it a family because here we find our identity. He called it a temple, because we're like pieces that come together, to build and hold up one another. He called it a flock of sheep because we are cared for by the same shepherd. And He called it a body because we're all different parts and no purpose or function is like the other. He called it His bride because the church is the love of His life.

It's a place where we grow into the fullness of Christlikeness.

3 Read Hebrews 10:24–25 and Proverbs 17:17.

Who is someone who spurs you on toward love and good deeds?

Who is someone who sharpens your faith?

How would your life be different without these people?

Who is someone you can encourage toward love, good deeds, and sharpening their faith?

4 Read Ephesians 4:31-32. What does Paul instruct believers?

How do these practices help foster health in a Christ-centered community?

Which of these practices is easiest for you and which is hardest?

Reflecting on all these passages, why do you think community is such an important part of God's plan to save the world?

Call to Action

Team up with someone in your group (or online if you are doing this study virtually) and share in a nutshell one or two hurts or hang-ups you have when it comes to being part of a community and the church. Spend some time praying for healing for each other. Then discuss one invitation in life you need to say yes to and one person whom you can make an invitation to this week.

Conclusion

Group leader, read aloud to the group to close your time together this week.

It's tempting to believe the lie that we're better off trying to do life on our own. Believing this falsehood creates a sense of false safety and stunts our spiritual growth. God makes it clear that we are better together.

No matter what pain or disappointment we've experienced in the past, God wants to bring healing and wholeness to our present. Growing in community is possible! It begins with saying yes to the invitations in front of us and issuing invitations to the people before us. As we come together in community and in unity through God's church, we declare God's power and presence to the world.

Closing Prayer

Select a volunteer to read the closing prayer over the group.

Forgive us for any time we've believed the lie that we're better off on our own. Help us to engage in the community you're calling us into more deeply. Bring new people into our lives to build meaningful friendships and also strengthen the friendships we already have. Empower us, through your Spirit, to walk in love and unity. May we, together, share the good news of Christ to the world. Amen.

Between Sessions

Personal Study

Check in with your group members during the upcoming week and continue the discussion you had with them at your last gathering. Grab coffee, dinner, or reach out by text and share what's going on in your life and heart. Use the following questions to help guide your conversation.

Community can be a difficult thing. Sometimes when we try to be part of a community, we run into people who make us feel less than or excluded. We encounter people who speak one way to our faces and another way behind our backs. We hold high expectations that are met with disappointment. And sometimes we're left wondering if we even want to make ourselves vulnerable again.

This week's group discussion is just the start, and the goal is to keep digging into how you can share God's love with the people right next to you. This section is created as a guide for your personal study time to further explore the topics you discussed with your group. If you're following along with the book for the fullest experience of this message, read or review chapters 10–12 in *How (Not) to Save the World*.

1 **On the continuum below, mark how much you struggle with letting people into your life.**

I don't struggle at all.

It's an everyday battle.

2 When have you most recently resisted letting people in?

3 Where do you think this stems from in your childhood or life experience?

4 **Mark any of the following steps which would be helpful as you heal from past hurts.**

____ Talking to a leader or mentor

____ Confiding the hurt to a friend

____ Looking up Scripture about healing

____ Talking to God about it

____ Prayerfully journaling the experience

____ Asking God to help you forgive

____ Asking for prayer about this hurt

____ Exploring the issue with a professional counselor

____ Celebrating a life-long friendship you enjoy

____ Other_____

How can you engage in the activities you selected this week?

The Bible is full of wisdom, guidance, and instruction on how to be part of a flourishing community.

5 **Read 1 Thessalonians 5:14. What three instructions are given regarding engaging others? Write them in the space below.**

- _____

- _____

- _____

Rank these in order of which comes most naturally and which is most challenging for you.

6 **Take a moment to ask God for someone whom you can serve in these ways. Write his or her name in the space below.**

Then take a moment to send a quick text or email to serve and love that person.

Whenever you engage in relationships, sooner or later there will be moments of misunderstanding, lack of communication, and mistakes made. It's not a question of if these things will happen, but when. And more importantly, the response given.

7 **Read Ephesians 4:26–27 and Colossians 3:13. What are the benefits of forgiving others quickly?**

Why is forgiveness crucial to healthy Christ-centered community?

Who is one person who you are particularly angry with right now?

Name: _____

How will you forgive the person and perhaps make the relationship right?

Who is one person you suspect is frustrated or angry with you?

Name: _____

How will you reach out, ask for forgiveness, and make the relationship right?

8 **Read Romans 12:3-8. What gifts do you bring to the community of believers?**

How frequently do you share or use your gifts within the community of believers?

How is the community of the Church better because of your gifts?

How would the community of the Church suffer from lack of using your gifts?

Who can you encourage to use their gifts within their community?

Name: _____

9 **Read Romans 12:9–13. In the space below, write out the instructions in this passage. Then circle the one(s) that you sense the Holy Spirit nudging you to do this week.**

We can be the *change* we long to see in the church. We can show people the *beauty* of the family of God.

In chapter 10 of *How (Not) to Save the World*, "Always Fly Solo," Hosanna writes the following reminder:

> *The church is Jesus' plan to reach a world that desperately needs Him. The lost have hope through it. The hurt are healed through it. We must love and forgive and fight to protect it because the community of the church is His absolute favorite. Alone, we cannot expect to be victorious in our battle against darkness. Alone, we cannot expect to stand tall through raging storms. Alone, we can't expect to rebuild our cities and restore our communities. To walk in our purposes and to stay on mission, we must walk with other people and stay in community. The more unified we are, the greater our impact will be.*

Write a prayer on the lines below asking God to help you see the church from His perspective. Write down anything that comes to mind.

_____

_____

_____

_____

_____

_____

_____

_____

_____

_____

_____

_____

_____

⑩ Before your next group meeting, read chapters 13–14 if you are reading along with the book.

Never Giving Up

With all of your heart and your time and your life, *you must do* what God has called *you* to do. Fight the battles God has called *you* to fight.

—Hosanna Wong
From Chapter 13 of *How (Not) to Save the World*

Opening Discussion

1 Who is someone in your life you have prayed for or hoped would know Christ for a long time?

2 On a scale of one to ten, how hopeful are you that this person will discover Jesus?

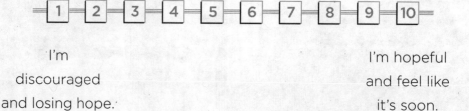

I'm discouraged and losing hope.

I'm hopeful and feel like it's soon.

3 Do you have any people in your life that you've given up hope on and think they will never discover Jesus?

If so, what has caused you to give up hope? What would renew your hope?

Session 5 Video (26 minutes)

As you watch, take notes on anything that stands out to you.

NOTES:

▶ I ministered to my brother so wrong

▶ Lie: Always fight to be right

▶ Learn the words and ways of those around us and of God

▶ People want to be seen, known, and know they are not alone

▶ Jesus sat with Judas

▶ Jesus has already saved the world, but the mission isn't finished

Hosanna shares how no one processes grief or loss the same way. After her father passed away, she told her brother that God didn't want him to be sad and that he just needed to have more faith. This did more harm than good.

1️⃣ Describe a time when you were suffering or in pain and someone spoke harmful or hurtful words to you. Then describe a time when you were suffering or in pain and someone spoke helpful and healing words to you.

2️⃣ What made the difference between those two experiences?

3️⃣ How have those experiences shaped the way you respond to others who are hurting?

Hosanna teaches, "Do you know why your neighbors struggle with the idea of church and how they've been hurt in the past? Do you know why your family member doesn't want to share about their life or doesn't feel welcomed? Do you know whom your baby brother's favorite superhero is? When you ask great questions, listen well, and live in a consistent, real relationship, you will learn their words and ways, and know better how to respond."

4️⃣ How does understanding others' backstories and wounds help us have more compassion?

5️⃣ Discuss someone you've been frustrated or put off with (no need to say the name aloud) but who learning more about might create more compassion and connection.

What are some gentle, good questions you could ask?

6 **Whom do you most need to love right now, right where he or she is?**

Bible Study Connection

Group leader, read the following comments to the group and then read the associated Bible passage aloud, followed by further discussion questions.

1 **Read 2 Corinthians 5:20.**

What does it mean to represent Christ in this way?

When do you struggle most to represent Christ in this way?

Discuss which comes more easily for you: knowing the words and ways of others or knowing the words and ways of God.

What are the best practices for really getting to know others and understanding their stories?

What are the best practices for really getting to know the Bible and answers to the spiritual questions people are asking?

2 **Read Romans 5:8.**

When did God demonstrate His love?

How can you show God's love to others and step into their world before they step into yours?

3 **Read Galatians 6:9.**

Where are you most weary in your spiritual journey?

Where are you most weary when it comes to sharing Christ with someone you love?

What hope do you find in this passage as well as in Hosanna's story of her brother?

4 **Reflect on how your attitude toward sharing your faith has changed since you started this study.**

What have you learned about sharing your story and talking about Jesus?

How have you become more intentional about sharing your faith?

Where do you see evidence of growth and discovery as you review your notes, notes, and reflections?

What is the biggest takeaway for you from this study?

Call to Action

Team up with someone in your group (or online if you are doing this study virtually) and share some of the story of the person who you most want to know Christ. Take a moment to pray for their salvation.

Conclusion

Group leader, read aloud to the group to close your time together this week.

Instead of fighting to be right, we need to fight for our relationships. We are the ambassadors of Christ and to represent Him well, we need to learn the words and ways of others and the words and ways of God. Though we may grow weary waiting for those we love to know Jesus, we must persevere in prayer, and never give up.

Closing Prayer

Select a volunteer to read the closing prayer over the group.

Thank you for this opportunity to gather and for all we've learned through our time together. As your ambassadors, help us to represent you well and love others the way you love them. Strengthen our resolve to persevere in patience, prayer, and never giving up. Amen.

Between Sessions
Personal Study

To reach her brother, Hosanna says she started reading comic books and watching endless superhero movies. "I was able to connect with Elijah through stepping into his world and starting to see it the way he saw it and eventually speaking to him where he really was."

1 **Describe a time when you were hurting and someone expressed genuine, above-and-beyond love for you.**

What did that look and feel like?

This week's group discussion is just the start, and the goal is to keep digging into how you can share God's love with the people right next to you. This section is created as a guide for your personal study time to further explore the topics you discussed with your group as well as reflect on what you've learned throughout the study.

2 Who is someone you know who is hurting for whom you can express genuine, above-and-beyond love?

Name: _____

What will you do for that person?

3 Read Matthew 26:17–30. How does Jesus choose to spend the final hours with His disciples before His arrest?

Among those sitting with Jesus, who would soon betray, deny, or leave Him? (hint v. 47–50, 56, and 69–75)

What does this reveal about Jesus' love for His disciples?

Why does Jesus refuse to give up on the disciples?

What does this passage reveal about Jesus' refusal to give up on you and those you love?

How do you feel about sharing your faith now that you have completed this study?

What Bible passage has empowered you most when it comes to sharing your faith?

How has your relationship with God changed during this study?

In the opening session, you were asked the following question:

Who are three people right front of you—on your street, in your apartment building, at school pick up, in a nearby cubicle, in your family, on a walking path—with whom you've overlooked and can begin building relationships?

3 How have your relationships with these people changed during this study?

*N*ever give up on your loved ones.

In conclusion of *How (Not) to Save the World*, "How Jesus Saved the World," Hosanna writes the following reminder:

> *I look forward to being on this mission alongside of you. Eating the best meals, taking some big steps of faith, fumbling here and there but being rescued through it all. Going to art festivals, reading comic books, having more random but life-giving relationships that we've ever imagined, and sharing the hope of Jesus with those right next to us.*
>
> *Together.*
>
> *Sharing all our stories.*
>
> *Sitting at all the tables.*
>
> *Opening all the doors.*

4 **What's one thing you never knew about sharing your faith that you know now?**

How has that knowledge impacted you?

Meet Hosanna Wong

Hosanna Wong is an international speaker, bestselling author, and spoken-word artist empowering this generation to know who they are and boldly live out their purpose. Hosanna speaks in churches, conferences, prisons, and other events around the world year-round. She and her husband, Guy, serve in various ministries, equipping the local and global church.

More information at www.hosannawong.com

COMPANION BOOK TO ENRICH YOUR STUDY EXPERIENCE

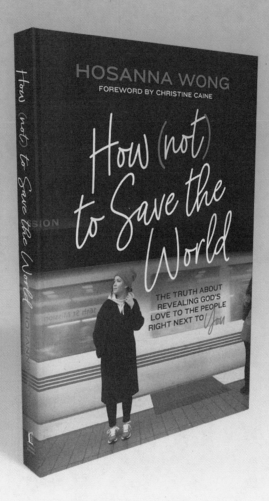

ISBN 9780785243021

Available wherever books are sold

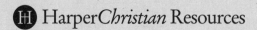

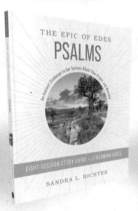

From the Publisher

GREAT STUDIES

ARE EVEN BETTER WHEN THEY'RE SHARED!

Help others find this study:

- Post a review at your favorite online bookseller.

- Post a picture on a social media account and share why you enjoyed it.

- Send a note to a friend who would also love it—or, better yet, go through it with them!

Thanks for helping others grow their faith!